LIFE COACHING SUCCESSFUL MEN

THE

SUPER

MAN

YOU ARE BOUND FOR GREATNESS

Theodore Baxter

Table of Contents

PART 1 5

Chapter 1: Why You Need To Find Your Why..............................6

Chapter 2: How to Love Yourself First 9

Chapter 3: How To Deal With Uncertainty?...............................12

Chapter 4: Happy People Are Optimistic.....................................15

Chapter 5: How to Identify the Obstacles Holding You Back.....20

Chapter 6: *How to Face Difficulties in Life*.................................26

Chapter 7: Get Rid of Worry and Focus On The Work 30

Chapter 8: Feeling Lost In Life 33

Chapter 9: *Motivation With Good Feelings*...................................36

Chapter 10: Overcoming the Fear of Failure 39

PART 2 42

Chapter 1: It's Not Your Job to Tell Yourself "No" 43

Chapter 2: *What To Do When You Feel Like Your Work is not Good Enough*
....46

Chapter 3: How To Rid Yourself of Distraction.........................50

Chapter 4: Dealing With Inertia (Gym) Motivation....................53

Chapter 5: *The People You Need in Your Life*..............................56

Chapter 6: Why You Are Setting The Wrong Goals....................59

Chapter 7: The Power of Developing Eye Contact with Your Client...63

Chapter 8: Don't Fear Judgement...66

Chapter 9: 4 Ways to Deal with Feelings of Inferiority When
Comparing to Others...69

Chapter 10: Why Are You Working So Hard 71

PART 3 74

Chapter 1: 8 Ways To Love Yourself First...................................75

Chapter 2: 8 Ways to Discover What's holding You Back From
Achieving Your Visions..79

Chapter 3: 6 Steps To Get Out of Your Comfort Zone 83

Chapter 4: 7 Ways To Develop Effective Communication With Your Clients 89

Chapter 5: 6 Ways to Start All Over Again 94

Chapter 6: 6 Ways On How To Change Your Body Language To Attract Success 98

Chapter 7: 5 Ways To Adopt Right Attitude For Success 102

Chapter 8: 5 Lessons on Being Wrong 106

Chapter 9: Five Steps to Clarify Your Goals 110

Chapter 10: Consistency Can Bring You Happiness 113

PART 1

Chapter 1:

Why You Need To Find Your Why

Your why is your reason for being.

Your reason for living.

Your reason for acting.

Without a why life begins to feel demoralising.

Without a purpose, what is the purpose?

What chance do you think you have of achieving anything, without a reason?

Go out and ask 20 people why they are working, apart from the pay.

Roughly 16 will not be able to give you a clear answer, and 4 will.

The 4 that will have a plan and a goal to achieve more.

They probably already are more successful than the 16 with no answer.

The 4 know their current work is just a step to a bigger goal.

They know their what and their why behind everything they are doing.

The 16 just landed in that job by chance and will probably never leave it.

They may progress up the company ladder slowly,

But with no clear reason to achieve anything greater they will stay where they are,

in perceived security.

Do you know why you are doing what you are doing?

If not, it's about time you discover your why.

It may be to providing a better life for your family and friends.

Your motives may be financial, they may not.

Maybe your why is to lead a less stressful life.

Maybe that means your require less money to be happy.

Your reason is individual and personal.
No one else should influence that.
Seek to heed advice from people who are where you want to be in life.
You wouldn't let a mechanic perform surgery on you,
so why would you accept advice on success from the unsuccessful.

They may be successful in their field.
But if their field is not your field, they have no business telling you how to play.
Their why is not your why, and their what is not your what.
If the goals and reasons are different, the advice is irrelevant.

Politely respect their advice.
Use their success to fuel your drive for success in your own field.
Help it guide you to a similar path that you are aiming towards.

Your why is so important.
It will be the reason you persist when things get tough.
If you have no clearly defined reason, it becomes easy for you to quit.

A clearly defined goal (your what),
and a clearly defined reason (your why),
are critical to any lasting happiness and success.
Without them you are just aimlessly drifting from nothing to nothing.
Without clearly defining the terms of your life , you forfeit the power of your will
and your life will be decided by someone else.
That is tragedy.

Your why truly is everything on the path to achieving your what.
Your end goal.
Your dream life.

Everything that you will sit down and clearly define.

The detail of everything and the people who will enjoy it - your ultimate why.

What and why go together like salt and pepper or bread and butter.

You can't have one without the other.

Chapter 2:

How to Love Yourself First

It's so easy to tell someone "Love yourself" and much more difficult to describe *how* to do it. Learn and practice these six steps to gradually start loving yourself more every day:

Step 1: Be willing to feel pain and take responsibility for your feelings.

Step 1 is mindfully following your breath to become present in your body and embrace all of your feelings. It's about moving toward your feelings rather than running away from them with various forms of self-abandonment, such as staying focused in your head, judging yourself, turning to addictions to numb out, etc. All feelings are informational.

Step 2: Move into the intent to learn.

Commit to learning about your emotions, even the ones that may be causing you pain, so that you can move into taking loving action.

Step 3: Learn about your false beliefs.

Step 3 is a deep and compassionate process of exploration—learning about your beliefs and behavior and what is happening with a person or situation that may be causing your pain. Ask your feeling self, your inner child: "What am I thinking or doing that's causing the painful feelings of anxiety, depression, guilt, shame, jealousy, anger, loneliness, or emptiness?" Allow the answer to come from inside, from your intuition and feelings.

Once you understand what you're thinking or doing that's causing these feelings, ask your ego about the fears and false beliefs leading to the self-abandoning thoughts and actions.

Step 4: Start a dialogue with your higher self.

It's not as hard to connect with your higher guidance as you may think. The key is to be open to learning about loving yourself. The answers may come immediately or over time. They may come in words or images or dreams. When your heart is open to learning, the answers will come.

Step 5: Take loving action.

Sometimes people think of "loving myself" as a feeling to be conjured up. A good way to look at loving yourself is by emphasizing the action: "What can I *do* to love myself?" rather than "How can I *feel* love for myself?"

By this point, you've already opened up to your pain, moved into learning, started a dialogue with your feelings, and tapped into your spiritual guidance. Step 5 involves taking one of the loving actions you identified in Step 4. However small they may seem at first, over time, these actions add up.

Step 6: Evaluate your action and begin again as needed.

Once you take the loving action, check in to see if your pain, anger, and shame are getting healed. If not, you go back through the steps until you discover the truth and loving actions that bring you peace, joy, and a deep sense of intrinsic worth.

Over time, you will discover that loving yourself improves everything in your life—your relationships, health and well-being, ability to manifest your dreams, and self-esteem. Loving and connecting with yourself is the key to loving and connecting with others and creating loving relationships. Loving yourself is the key to creating a passionate, fulfilled, and joyful life.

Chapter 3:

How To Deal With Uncertainty?

How many of you are going through life right now but are dealing with a load of uncertainty that is weighing heavily on your mind?

You could be worrying about your career or work related matters: you wonder because the economy is taking a hit, whether you will still have your job tomorrow, whether your business would survive, or even if the economy is good, you are uncertain if you quit the current job you hate whether you are able to find another job in the near future or if you will even be competent in your new profession.

Or you could be worrying about your loved ones, your child who is studying overseas, or your spouse where they are working in the healthcare profession, working in the police or fire department, or even the military, where their lives are put at risk every single day, you worry if there will be one day that you might lose them and they won't come home.

Or you could be uncertain about smaller matters, matters such as if your date went well and if they would give you a call to ask you out again.

Whatever these may be, they all fall under the umbrella of uncertainty.

I would like to share with you uncertainties I faced personally and I would like to provide you with action steps to deal with them.

Recently I had been struggling with many uncertainties in my life. While they might not be your struggles I believe I would be able to provide more value if i shared my own story.

The first uncertainty I had was that I had recently restarted my publishing business after being away from it for a year, I was so afraid of what the market condition was like now, I was afraid of the competition, I was afraid I would fail again. I was afraid I would waste more of my time building up a business only to have it taken away from me.

The second worry I had was that I had also just begun taking my real estate exam to become a licensed realtor. I started having doubts about myself that I would ever become a competent realtor like my peers and I would look like a fool and I would feel disappointed with myself thereafter.

The next uncertainty I had was whether I would get the jobs that I applied for. I had decided to take on a part or full-time position to grow my professional career and I was afraid Whether the hours I spent on job applications would be in vain and that i would get no responses or even worse, rejections.

The final uncertainty was with stocks. Due to the incredible market volatility, I couldn't sleep properly every night because I wasn't sure what was gonna happen tmr. Whether I was gonna lose money while i was asleep.

I went about days with all these negative thoughts looming in my mind. It affected my sleep, my well-being, and my happiness. I started becoming dreary, unhappy, and lifeless. I spent 80% of my waking hours with these fears and doubts, and constantly beating myself up for feeling this way and it only made matters worse.

One day I decided it was enough. I took a deep breath and started collecting myself. I had had enough and I was so done with feeling these uncertainty and feeling sorry for myself.

I made the decision to accept my struggles, that they were a part of life and that there was no point in worrying about it. I decided it that I would just work hard on these areas, keep doing my best, and that whatever outcomes doesn't matter because I've given it my all. And finally I decided to live my day to the fullest and just be grateful that I even get to have the opportunity to pursue these ventures. After going through this process day in and day out, I became more at peace with myself. I started feeling less anxiety and adopted a more optimistic and positive mindset.

Here's what I realized. Uncertainty is born out of fear. This could be fear of losing someone, fear of the unknown, or even fear of failure. I had immense fears of failure that it crippled me to a really low point in my life. And the only way to overcome fear is first to accept that it is normal to be fearful, and then after to not let that fear get in the way of your happiness because life is too short for you to spend in a state of fearfulness. Rather, spend your time feeling grateful for your life and just try your best in everything that you do. Keep working on your dreams as if it were your last day on this earth, keep loving your spouse or child as though it was their last day on this earth, and ask yourself, is this how you would want to spend your time letting fear and uncertainty feed on your happiness? Or would you rather cherish every single moment you have with yourself and your family, and to live life with abundance instead.

This is my challenge to you. Uncertainty can only cripple you if you let it. Focus on your journey, your path, and trust in the process. But most importantly, Trust in yourself, believe in yourself even if no one else will. You owe that much love and compassion to yourself. I know you can do it.

Chapter 4:

Happy People Are Optimistic

Beyond the simple reality that optimists are happier people (and happiness is what you're striving for), optimism has other benefits as well. So, if you want to achieve greater happiness, try being optimistic for a day.

Optimists enjoy a greater degree of academic success than pessimists do. Because optimistic students think it's possible for them to make a good grade, they study hardier and they study smarter. They manage the setting in which they study and they seek help from others when they need it. (Optimism, it turns out, is almost as predictive of how well students do in college as the SAT.)

Optimists are more self-confident than pessimists are. They believe in *themselves* more than fate.

Optimists are more likely to be problem-solvers than pessimists are. When pessimistic students get a D on a test, they tend to think things like: "I knew I shouldn't have taken this course. I'm no good at psychology." The optimistic student who gets a D says to herself, "I can do better. I just didn't study enough for this test. I'll do better next time." And she will.

Optimists welcome second chances after they fail more than pessimists do. Optimistic golfers always take a *mulligan* (a redo swing without penalty). Why? Because they expect to achieve a better result the second time around.

Optimists are more socially outgoing than pessimists are. Socially outgoing folks believe that the time they spend with other human beings makes them better in some way — smarter, more interesting, more attractive. Unfortunately, pessimists see little, if any, benefit from venturing out into the social world.

Optimists are not as lonely as pessimists are. Because pessimists don't see as much benefit from socializing with others, they have far fewer social and emotional connections in their lives, which is what loneliness is all about.

Optimists utilize social support more effectively than pessimists do. They aren't afraid to reach out in times of need.

Optimists are less likely to blame others for their misfortune than pessimists are. When you blame someone else for your troubles, what you're really saying is, "You're the *cause* of my problem and, therefore, you have to be the *solution* as well." Optimists have just as many troubles as pessimists throughout life — they just accept more responsibility for dealing with their misfortune.

Optimists cope with stress better than pessimists do. Pessimists worry, optimists act. A patient with coronary heart disease who is pessimistic "hopes and prays" that he doesn't have another heart attack anytime soon. The optimistic heart patient leaves little to chance — instead, he exercises regularly, practices his meditation exercises, adheres to a low-cholesterol diet, and makes sure he always gets a good night's sleep.

How to Stop Chasing New Goals All the Time

The philosopher Alan Watts always said that life is like a song, and the sole purpose of the song is to dance. He said that when we listen to a song, we don't dance to get to the end of the music. We dance to enjoy it. This isn't always how we live our lives. Instead, we rush through our moments, thinking there's always something better, there's always some goal we need to achieve.

"Existence is meant to be fun. It doesn't go anywhere; it just is." Our lives are not about things and status. Even though we've made ourselves miserable with wanting, we already have everything we need. Life is meant to be lived. If you can't quit your job tomorrow, enjoy where you are. Focus on the best parts of every day. Believe that everything you do has a purpose and a place in the world.

Happiness comes from gratitude. You're alive, you have people to miss when you go to work, and you get to see them smile every day. We all have to do things we don't want to do; we have to survive. When you find yourself working for things that don't matter, like a big house or a fancy car, when you could be living, you've missed the point. You're playing the song, but you're not dancing.

"A song isn't just the ending. It's not just the goal of finishing the song. The song is an experience."

We all think that everything should be amazing when we're at the top, but it's not. Your children have grown older, and you don't remember the little things.

"...tomorrow and plans for tomorrow can have no significance at all unless you are in full contact with the reality of the present since it is in the present and only in the present that you live."

You feel cheated of your time, cheated by time. Now you have to make up for it. You have to live, make the most of what you have left. So you set another goal.

This time you'll build memories and see places, do things you never got the chance to do. The list grows, and you wonder how you'll get it all done and still make your large mortgage payment. You work more hours so you can do all this stuff "someday." You've overwhelmed yourself again.

You're missing the point.

Stop wanting more, <u>be grateful for</u> today. Live in the moment. Cherish your life and the time you have in this world. If it happens, it happens. If it doesn't, then it wasn't meant to; let it go.

"We think if we don't interfere, it won't happen."

There's always an expectation, always something that has to get done. You pushed aside living so that you could live up to an expectation that doesn't exist to anyone but you. The expectation is always there because you gave it power. To live, you've got to let it go.

You save all your money so that you can retire. You live to retire. Then you get old, and you're too tired to live up to the expectation you had of retirement; you never realize your dreams.

At forty, you felt cheated; at eighty, you are cheated. You cheated yourself the whole way through to the end.

"Your purpose was to dance until the end, but you were so focused on the end that you forgot to dance."

Chapter 5:

How to Identify the Obstacles Holding You Back

Hi everyone! Have you ever wanted something in your life so badly but you failed to take any action to get it? Did you ever find out what was holding you back?

As humans, we have lots of aspirations and dreams. We strive to be rich and successful, pursuing our passions, having a big family, and living in a nice house with our dream car.
But how many of us were able to chase down that dream?

In today's video, we're going to talk about just that.

Let's find out how you can identify the obstacles holding us back from achieve your goals and how you can overcome them.

Before we begin, I would like you to first think about a goal you've been wanting to achieve but haven't started working on. If you're insightful, then ask yourself what are the possible reasons holding you back from working on it. Why are you procrastinating? Now that you've got something to latch on to, we can start to deconstruct the issues you might be facing.

1. Fear of Failure

Most of the time, fear holds us back. Fear of failure is the most common fear that stops many people, including you and me, from working towards our intended goals.

We are so afraid to fail after putting in an enormous amounts of time and effort, but we fail to realise that falling down is part of the process to victory. We do not see the struggles that many successful people have had to go through to get to where they are today – we only see the dollar signs that are tied to their name, their net-worth, their fancy houses and cars, things that are on face value. But in reality, they have had to fail their way to success. And we are oblivious to their trials and tribulations, their mindset, their incredible work ethic, and their ability to get themselves back up after falling flat on their faces and try again.

2. Fear of Change

Another fear that could be holding you back from taking action is the fear of change. You may find it challenging to go out of your comfort zones to explore the big world of possibilities waiting for you. You may find your current position very safe, warm, and cosy. No stress, no pressure, just simply fine. But there's no growth in your comfort zone.

I am here to tell you that going out there to try new things isn't going to be easy. There may be a steep learning curve and a huge mountain waiting for you to climb. Are you willing to step out of that perfectly warmed home into a blizzard outside?

Putting yourself in uncomfortable situations is the only way that you will face challenges that might prove to be rewarding in the long run. Changes that will give you new perspectives and teach you new lessons that you wouldn't have learnt otherwise if you merely stay in your safe zone. So don't be afraid to go out in the world and try new things. No matter what the outcome is, the experiences you'll gain along the way will always be priceless.

3. Fear of Judgement

Fear of being judged for doing things that are out of the norm is something that many of us are afraid of. In today's world, society has created a frame and a timeline of what seems to be pleasing and acceptable. Without realising it, we have been gradually moulded by society to try our best to blend into the crowd, not stand out. You may also inevitably feel that same pressure to simply just fit in. This irrational fear of being judged by others, whether it be our friends, family members, or even complete strangers, stops us in doing what we really want to do.

Now try to imagine yourself in a situation where other people won't judge you no matter what your dreams are. Instead, they will celebrate you for taking action and chasing your passions in life. If that were the reality, what will you do?

By reframing our thoughts, instead of succumbing to our desires of trying please everyone around us, we are thinking for ourselves first for once. There is no fear of judgement of pursuing what really matters to us. Don't be afraid to go out of that frame and restart. Listen to your own intuition and don't let the world put your hands on you and crush your dreams.

4. Fear of Making Mistakes

Are you the kind that always aces your test at school when you were young without studying? Or did you do well in school because you practiced a thousand times over before finally getting it right when it comes exam time?

You might think that having the perfect plan or having the perfect strategy is essential before you can begin executing your dreams, but in reality, a lot of the success only comes over time after many trials and errors. We have to keep the mindset that we will figure things out along the way as we travel down that new path. The journey will not be smooth sailing no matter how perfect we can try to make our plans to be. As with failures, making mistakes is part of the game. It is how you react to and manage the problems that come up that will be the true test of your capabilities.

Perfectionism is a trap that stops us from doing what we want. Doing something imperfectly is so much better than not doing anything at all because of the fear of imperfection.

5. Having a Weak Mindset

Another factor that holds people back is their own mindset. Have you ever wanted to try something out but you instantly think that you can't do it? The thought that you are incapable of something is all in your mind. You must tell yourself that you are flexible and fluid. That you are able to achieve anything you set your mind to.

That you have what it takes to go after the life that you want. The truth is, you have everything within you to be successful if you'll just believe that you can. Every time you catch yourself thinking that you can't be who you want to be, the reality is not that you can't do it, but rather that you just simply don't want to do it – either out of laziness or out of the fears that we have described so far.

To change your life you first have to change your mindset and be open to all possibilities.

6. Blaming Others Your Shortcomings

It is human nature to blame others for things that we lack or fail to do. We may direct our failure to take action to our circumstances, our environment, our lack of resources, or even our parents.

Blaming everything and everyone around you for your circumstances will hinder you from moving forward. Instead, be accountable for your own progress. We all have a choice to look at ourselves first and find the shortcomings that we may have. It could be a lack of motivation, lack of perseverance, , lack of patience, lack of consistency, and lack of discipline that is holding you back.

It is time to stop looking at external factors as reasons for our inability to take action. We all need to start working on ourselves first before we can see real change and progress happen to our lives. If you don't want where you are right now, do something about it. Move heaven and earth if you must. Don't stop until you reach where you want to be.

Knowing what's holding you back is the first step you need to take to overcome them. Acknowledge these blockers and work on them. If you are afraid to fail, remember that failure is just part of the whole journey. If you are afraid of the uncertainties, remember that all our choices are half chances. And if we are afraid that we might just be wasting time, remember that whatever the outcome that your learning and experiences will make all your effort worth it in the end. You are not defined by the amount of effort you put in, not your failures.

I hope this video inspires you to always choose to look at things positively and outgrow whatever hinders you. No matter what your circumstances are, you have the power to turn things around and succeed. Many people have done it and trust that you can also do it. If you like this video, please give it a thumbs up and subscribe for more.

Happy People Dream Big

Remember being a kid, and when somebody asked you what you wanted to be after growing up, you answered with a big dream: an astronaut, a ballerina, a scientist, a firefighter, or the President of the United States. You believed that you could achieve anything you set your mind at that no dream is too big that if you wanted, you would make it happen. But why is it that so many adults forget what it is like to dream big. Happy people are dreamers; if you want to become a happy person, you need to make dreaming big a habit; some people even say that if your dreams do not scare you, you are not dreaming big. Now you must be wondering how dreaming big can make you happy. Firstly, it helps you see that if you had a magic wand and you could get whatever you wanted, what you would want for yourself, and there is a chance that these dreams are things you want to achieve in your life somehow other. Secondly, it will help you in removing any fears you have about not being able to achieve your dreams because when you dream big, you think about what you want in your ideal world, and your fear will not come in your way because you would feel like you are living in that fantasy world. Lastly, you will put your dreams and desires into the universe, and the likelihood of making those dreams come true increases. Fulfilling your dreams makes you happy because you will be able to get what you have yearned for so long, and a sense of achievement will make you feel confident about yourself and the dream you had. Now you must have a question what should I do to start dreaming big I am going to outline some of the things you can practice!

Sit back, clear your mind and think about your desires and dreams. What do you want in life? If you had three wishes from a genie, what are the things you would ask for? What is something you would if no one was looking or if you weren't afraid. Now write these dreams down on a piece of paper. This way, they would seem more real. The next thing you should do is start reading some inspirational books that motivate you to start living your best life starting today! Lastly, make a list of goals you want to achieve and start working on them.

Chapter 6:

How to Face Difficulties in Life

Have you noticed that difficulties in life come in gangs attacking you when you're least prepared for them? The effect is like being forced to endure an unrelenting nuclear attack.

Overcoming obstacles in life is hard. But life is full of personal challenges, and we have to summon the courage to face them. These test our emotional mettle — injury, illness, unemployment, grief, divorce, death, or even a new venture with an unknown future. Here are some strategies to help carry you through:

1. Turn Toward Reality

So often, we turn away from life rather than toward it. We are masters of avoidance! But if we want to be present—to enjoy life and be more effective in it—we must orient ourselves toward facing reality. When guided by the reality principle, we develop a deeper capacity to deal with life more effectively. What once was difficult is now easier. What once frightened us now feels familiar. Life becomes more manageable. And there's something even deeper that we gain: Because we can see that we have grown stronger, we have greater confidence that we can grow even stronger still. This is the basis of feeling capable, which is the wellspring of a satisfying life.

2. Embrace Your Life as It Is Rather Than as You Wish It to Be

The Buddha taught that the secret to life is to want what you have and do not want what you don't have. Being present means being present to the life that you have right here, right now. There is freedom in taking life as it comes to us—the good with the bad, the wonderful with the tragic, the love with the loss, and the life with the death. When we embrace it all, then we have a real chance to enjoy life, value our experiences, and mine the treasures that are there for the taking. When we surrender to the reality of who we are, we give ourselves a chance to do what we can do.

3. Take Your Time

As the story of the tortoise and the hare tells us, slow and steady wins the race. By being in a hurry, we actually thwart our own success. We get ahead of ourselves. We make more mistakes. We cut corners and pay for them later. We may learn the easy way but not necessarily the best way. As an old adage puts it: The slower you go, the sooner you get there. Slow, disciplined, incremental growth is the kind of approach that leads to lasting change.

<u>Gravitational Leadership</u>

Leadership.

It's not about position it is about disposition. It is not a title it is a role. A role you can take on from any place. Even if you are at the lowest point in the hierarchy – you can still lead. Leadership is not about being on the top rung, it is about holding ladders for others. It is not about having the most authority either. When a battalion went on a mission authorised by the King, the battalion did not have the King's authority, only his approval. Yet within them someone could still rise and lead the others. The beginning of your leadership is making decisions and taking action that gets approved by the people in authority. In doing that you will get noticed and over time trusted as an advisor. Sometimes the way you think and conduct yourself will enable you to lead people above you before you get any opportunity to lead people below you.

Because leadership is gravity.

Gravity does not push us downwards. It is not a force that comes from above us and holds us back.

Firstly, gravity does not push it pulls. Pulling involves leading by example and drawing people to you by virtue of your character. The good decisions that you make, the beneficial actions that you take, start to bundle together as a mass of admirable quality under your name. And gravity is just a reflection of mass. The more you engage and go all-in the faster that mass will grow – and with it your gravity will.

But gravity is not just something that attracts the people below you. Gravity doesn't pull downwards on a 2D plane, it pulls towards a centre. The people who are on the same level as you should be led by you as well. Not only that but you should be influencing the people above you.

Not in such a way that you suck up to them but in a way that you stand out. Not necessarily even with the intention of climbing the ladder. Leadership must always be about leading in the space that you are without leaning towards the space you want to be. Allow promotions or advancements to flow naturally – if you try to force them then you will be detracting from your gravity and ultimately end up worse off.

Lastly, gravity does not hold people back, it keeps them grounded. Gravity is the force that enables us to walk forward, to move while retaining control. People who have been to space can testify to the lack of control experienced without gravity and the dangers therein. The markings of a leader is someone who is able to keep people grounded to the mission while still giving them freedom of movement. Gravity does not inhibit progress it gives it a better framework to work within. It allows people to pursue things with passion while staying within the borders of a greater purpose.

Such is the makings of a leader.

Chapter 7:

Get Rid of Worry and Focus On The Work

Worry is the active process of bringing one's fears into reality.

Worrying about problems halts productivity by taking your mind off the work in hand.

If you're not careful, a chronic state of worrying can lead you down a dark path that you might find hard to get out of.

Always focus on the required work and required action towards your dream.

Anything could happen, good or bad,

but if you remain focused and do the work despite the problems,

you will through with persistence and succeed.

Always keep your mind on the goal,

your eyes on the prize.

Have an unwavering faith in your abilities no matter what.

Plan for the obvious obstacles that could stand in your way,

but never worry about them until you have to face them.

Tackle it with confidence as they come and move forward with pride.

Problems are bound to arise.

Respond to them necessarily along the way, if they actually happen.

After all, most worries never make it into reality.

Instead focus on what could go right.

Focus on how you can create an environment that will improve your chances of success.

You have the power over your own life and direction.

As children we dreamed big.

We didn't think about all the things that could go wrong.

As children we only saw the possibilities.

We were persistent in getting what we wanted no matter the cost.

As adults we need to be reminded of that child-like faith.

To crush worry as if it were never there.

To only focus on the possibilities.

You cannot be positive and negative at the same time.

You cannot be worrying and hopeful of the future.

You cannot visualise your perfect life while worrying about everything that could go wrong.

Choose one.

Stick to it.

Choose to concentrate on the work.

The result will take care of your worries.

Catch yourself when you feel yourself beginning to worry about things.

Instead of dwelling on the problem, choose to double down on the action.

Stay focused and steadfast in the vision of your ultimate goal.

The work now that you must do is the stepping stones to your success.

The work now must have your immediate attention.

The work now requires you to cast worry aside in favour of concentration and focus.

How many stepping stones are you away?

What is next?

Push yourself every single day.

Because only you have the power to create your future.

If not, things will remain the same as they have always been.

Always have a clearly defined goal,

A strong measure of faith,

And an equally strong measure of persistence and grit.

These are the ingredients to creating the life you want.

A life of lasting happiness and success.

Take control instead of accepting things as they are.

Reject anything else that is not the goal that you've set for yourself.

Whatever goal you set, ten times it, and focus on it every day.

The focus will keep your mind on the work until you succeed.

There will be no time to worry when you are too busy taking constant action.

Always have the belief In your heart and soul that you will succeed.

Never let a grain of doubt cast a shadow in your eventual path to victory.

Focus is key to all.

What you focus on, you will create.

Worrying is worse than useless,

it is DETRIMENTAL to your future.

Take control of your thoughts.

When worry pops it's ugly head, force it out with a positive thought of your future.

Don't let the negative illusions of worry live rent-free in your mind.

You are in control here.

Of what you watch,

What you read,

What you listen too

And what you think.

What you think of consistently will become.

Focus on what you want, and how to get there is crucial for lasting happiness and success.

Chapter 8:

Feeling Lost In Life

Today we're going to talk about the topic of feeling lost in life and not knowing what to do next. I hope that by the end of this video I will be able to inspire you to start looking for ways to move forward and get out of your feeling of being stuck.

Feeling lost in life is a thing that I think many of us will go through at one point in our lives. It usually hits us like a truck when something that we have been working on for an extended period of life comes crashing to an end. Whether that be a long-term relationship, a long-held career, a lost of a family member, or a lost of anything that we have dedicated huge amounts of our time on.

This feeling of being lost usually comes to us in the most unexpected ways when we are not prepared for it. We feel lost because we are not sure what comes after. We are unsure of the unknown, a place we have never thought to think about because we never expect it to happen to us.

There were many times in my life when feeling lost seems to hit me when I least expect it - the most notable one being when started my first business and it came crashing to a halt due to some reasons which I would not go into. That abrupt end to my first business took me by surprise and I suddenly felt lost and unsure of what to do next. Instead of feeling sorry for myself however I took it as a life lesson and decided to find out what my next path was. It took me almost a year to figure that out because I had not planned for this. There was no backup plan or side business that I could pour my time in. For a while I did feel like I was swimming in an ocean with no end in sight. It was only after a long and arduous swim did I finally find some dry land where I could set up camp again.

For those of us who have spent most of our early years working towards a degree that we think might be the end all be all career for us, we may find ourselves completely lost at sea as well when we find that our career no longer brings us joy but dread. Or that we find ourselves completely unsuited for this career and are nearing the end of its tolerance for the job. Or that we may suddenly be fired from our positions without warning. All these factors would be natural warrants for feeling lost because we have set the expectation to only work on this job and this job alone with no backup plan whatsoever. We may realise that we had not planned to pick up any new skills that would make us attractive for hire in another career, or that we may have no idea at all of what to do next.

Feeling lost in life, whatever the reasons may be, can be avoided if we think ahead far enough into the future. When we know the kind of life that we want to lead, the kind of income that we want to earn, we can be better prepared to make decisions today that would not land us in positions where a sudden loss of job will allow us to be thrown into the deep end of the pool. If we start to feel that something is amiss in our career, we may want to start doing some research early to see what other careers we may be able to plan for should we decide to quit our jobs. For most of us, we never want to find ourselves in a place where we have no career, no job, or no income. This sets off a wave of panic and fear in us that can lead us to feeling more lost and confused in life.

I believe the best way to avoid feeling lost is to never think of anything we have as permanent. We should not expect that the same job, career, or even person will be with us forever. We may want to consider starting a side stream of income so that we do not lay all our eggs in one basket. If something were to happen to our day jobs at least we can focus on our side business to tide us over until we can figure out what else to do next.

I have applied the same principle to all aspects of my life to avoid myself feeling lost. I have made it a point to have at least 5 areas that I could potentially work on should one or more than one fail. I never want to be in a position where my day job equals my livelihood. In that way I am forever bounded by 1 career and the fear of leaving or letting go would always be too great, not to mention the uncertainty in even keeping that one job in the first place.

Relationship wise and with dealing with loss and feeling lost without someone, of course I don't recommend you to have back-ups for those. I'm not into teaching polygamy or what not. In that sense it is absolutely and perfectly normal for us to simply go through the grieving process and hopefully move on with life. We may not be able to prepare for this but it could still happen to us. Remember that you should be self-sufficient first and foremost and that sometimes we may only be able to count on ourselves. We can't guarantee that the person we choose to love will be with us forever but we can only hope for that to be true.

So I challenge each and everyone of you to look ahead of you can. Always plan for failure and remember nothing ever stays the same. Do try to be prepared if somethings does not work out and shift your attention quickly to the next project especially with career and finance. As much as you can, don't ruminate on the loss but focus on the big picture. Hopefully with all these strategies I am able to help you not fall into the same trap as I did in feeling lost in life, that you will be better equipped to handle such shocking events.

I hope you learned something today. Take care and as always I'll see you in the next one.

Chapter 9:

Motivation With Good Feelings

Ever wonder what goes on in your mind when you feel depressed isn't always the reaction to the things that happen to you? What you go through when you feel down is the chemistry of your brain that you yourself allow being created in the first place.

You don't feel weak just because your heart feels so heavy. You feel weak because you have filled your heart with all these feelings that don't let you do something useful.

Feelings are not your enemy till you choose the wrong ones. In fact, Feelings and emotions can be the strongest weapon to have in your arsenal.

People say, "You are a man, so act like one. Men don't cry, they act strong and brave"

You must make yourself strong enough to overcome any feelings of failure or fear. Any thought that makes you go aloof and dims that light of creativity and confidence. It's OK to feel sad and cry for some time, but it's not OK to feel weak for even a second.

Your consciousness dictates your feelings. Your senses help you to process a moment and in turn help you translate them into feelings that go both ways. This process has been going on from the day you were born and will continue till your last day.

You enter your consciousness as soon as you open your eyes to greet the day. It is at this moment when your creativity is at its peak. What you need now is just a set of useful thoughts and emotions that steer your whole day into a worthwhile one.

Don't spend your day regretting and repressing things you did or someone else did to you. You don't need these feelings right now. Because you successfully passed those tests of life and are alive still to be grateful for what you have right now.

There are a billion things in life to be thankful for and a billion more to be sad for. But you cannot live a happy fulfilling life if you focus on the later ones.

Life is too short to be sad and to be weak. When you start your day, don't worry about what needs to be done. But think about who you need to be to get those things done.

Don't let actions and outcomes drive you. Be the sailor of yourself to decide what outcomes you want.

Believe me, the feeling of gratitude is the biggest motivator. Self gratitude should be the level of appraisal to expect. Nothing should matter after your own opinions about yourself.

If you let other people's opinions affect your feelings, you are the weakest person out there. And failure is your destination.

Visualization of a better life can help you feel and hope better. It would help you to grow stronger and faster but remember; The day you lose control of your emotions, feelings, and your temper, your imagination will only lead you to a downward spiral.

Chapter 10:

<u>Overcoming the Fear of Failure</u>

Stop it.

Stop whatever you are doing and take a moment to listen because you need to hear this...

Right now I want you to close your eyes and remember a time that you failed. I want you to remember how it made you feel. Remember the pain. Remember the guilt. Dig deep and remember the crushing weight of DISAPPOINTMENT that dragged you down to the depths of hell.

Do you feel it?! DO YOU REMEMBER THAT FEELING?! Good. Now get used to it - because you're gonna feel it again.

I need you to understand that failure is a part of life. In fact it's more than that. It's an essential part of life, of success! You think winners never failed? You think it's just you? Winners have failed more times than losers have ever TRIED!

People who succeed don't stop when they fail. They don't stop at ten, fifty or a hundred failures! They push through. They persevere. It doesn't matter how many times they get knocked down. They get right back up. Again. And again. And again. You know why? They don't fear failure.

Listen closely, because this will change your life. So long as you fear failure, you will never achieve success. You will never reach your dreams. Fearing failure is the only thing stopping you from becoming great. Greatness is a title reserved only for those who are willing to go head to head with failure - for those who face the fear of failure without hesitation! They look failure in the eye and say "I'll be damned if I let YOU sat and in my way!"

When they asked Michael Jordan how many shots he made, you know what he said? He told them they were nothing compared to how many he missed. Michael Jordan became the greatest basketball player of all time because he wasn't afraid to fail! What do you think would have happened if he had given up? If he had been scared to fail. He would never have become the legend that he did. He would have stayed a nobody - just like you.

Did that hurt? How did it make you feel? The pain. The guilt. The disappointment of knowing that so long as you fear failure YOU WILL BE A NOBODY. Your talent, your ability, the greatness within you! They will all die within you. If you aren't ready to accept that, then you need to make a change.

Get up. Get up from wherever you are hiding and face failure one on one. That fear is the only thing standing between you and success. You've got to get it through your head that this is it, the moment of truth. This is the time to decide who you are. Either you are a winner or a loser. If you can't look failure in the eye to achieve your dreams then you will never rise beyond mediocrity. But if you are a winner, now is the time to prove it. Forget mediocrity, you rise to the occasion. Failure is nothing more than one step closer to the greatness you desire. And if you can do that, if you can overcome the fear of failure... you can do anything.

PART 2

Chapter 1:

It's Not Your Job to Tell Yourself "No"

How many times have you had the chance to go around something that could have changed your life? What were your thoughts when you decided to enter a state where even the slightest thought of failure leads you to stop acting on it?

I'm sure every one of us has a good reason behind everything we opt to do or don't in our lives.

But there is never a good enough reason to back down just because we have some examples of failures on our hands.

No one can decide what reality and nature have decided for them. Everyone must learn to juggle life and play with every piece they get a hand on.

Everything in life is meant to be taken as a risk. You can never learn to swim till you get your first dive in a deep pool. You never learn to ride a bike till you have no one behind you to stop you from falling.

Everyone needs a bump every now and then. And when you finally decide to hike that hurdle, you finally start to see the horizon.

We all seem to get depressed more easily than we start to get motivated. We seem to get carried away with every stone that life throws back at us but we never try to catch that stone. We never try to indulge in one more suffering just to get better at what we are tested with.

Nobody wants to fail and that's why no one wants to take a chance at what might fail.

The mere fear of facing failure makes us build a mechanism of self-defense that forces us to say 'No' to anything that might hurt us one day.

But the reality is that it is illogical to stop just so you are afraid to face the reality. The reality is that you are a sane human and this is life. Life tests us in ways hardly imaginable.

When you say 'No' to yourself, it rarely means 'Not Now'. It always means 'Maybe some other time'. But deep down we already know that we will never attempt to do that thing. At least not consciously.

We always try for the best. We try to be the best at what we already have and are already doing. We are motivated enough to try new things, things that are more scary and unknown to us.

What we really should be doing is to try and get a taste of newer victories. Trying to search for new horizons. Trying to get what most fail to achieve. Because every other man or woman is just like us, afraid to fail and avoiding embarrassment. Our embarrassments are mostly self-imposed and we are the better judge of our failures.

There is no motivation and inspiration more powerful in the world than the spark that ignites within you.

Our sole purpose in life is to embrace everything that we come across. It is never to prevent something just because you don't have the courage to face your failures yet.

Chapter 2:

What To Do When You Feel Like Your Work is not Good Enough

Feeling like your work is not good enough is very common; your nerves can get better of you at any time throughout your professional life. There is nothing wrong with nerves; It tells you that you care about improving and doing well. Unfortunately, too much nervousness can lead to major self-doubt, and that can be crippling. You are probably very good at your work, and when even once you take a dip, you think that things are not like how they seem to you. If this is something you're feeling, then you're not alone, and this thing is known as Imposter Syndrome. This term is used to describe self-doubt and inadequacy. This one thing leaves people fearing that there might be someone who will expose them. The more pressure you apply to yourself, the more dislocation is likely to occur. You create more anxiety, which creates more fear, which creates more self-doubt. You don't have to continue like this. You can counter it.

Beyond Work

If your imposter syndrome affects you at work, you should take some time out and start focusing on other areas of your life. There are chances that there is something in your personal life that is hindering your work life. This could be anything your sleep routine, friends, diet, or even your relationships. There is a host of external factors that can affect your performance. If there are some boxes you aren't ticking, then there is a high chance of you not performing well at work.

You're Better Than You Think

When you're being crippled by self-doubt, the first thing you have to think about is why you were hired in the first place. The interviewers saw something in you that they believed would improve the business.

So, do you think they would recruit someone who can't do the job? No, they saw your talent, they saw something in you, and you will come good.

When you find yourself in this position, take a moment to write down a few things that you believe led to you being in the role you are now. What did those recruiters see? What did your boss recognize in you? You can also look back on a period of time where you were clicking and felt victorious. What was different then versus now? Was there an external issue like diet, exercise, socializing, etc.?

Check Yourself Before You Wreck Yourself

A checklist might be of some use to you. If you have a list to measure yourself against, then it gives you more than just one thing to judge yourself against. We're far too quick to doubt ourselves and criticize harshly.

The most obvious checklist in terms of work is technical or hard skills, but soft skills matter, too. It's also important to remember that while you're technically proficient now, things move quickly, and you'll reach a point where everything changes, and you have to keep up. You might not ever excel at something, but you can accept the change and adapt to the best of your ability.

It matters that you're hard-working, loyal, honest, and trustworthy. There's more to judge yourself on than just your job. Even if you make a mistake, it's temporary, and you can fix it.

Do you take criticism well? Are you teachable? Easy to coach? Soft skills count for something, which you can look to even at your lowest point and recognize you have strengths.

When you're struggling through a day, week, or even a month, take one large step backward and think about what it is you're unhappy with. What's causing your unhappiness, and how can you improve it?

It comes down to how well you know yourself. If you're clear on what your values are and what you want out of life, then you're going to be fine. If the organization you work for can't respect your values and harness your strengths, then you're better off elsewhere. So, it is extremely important to take time out for that self check-in there could be times you talk to yourself in negative light. Checking in with yourself regularly and not feeding yourself negativity could be one-step forward.

Chapter 3:

How To Rid Yourself of Distraction

Distraction and disaster sound rather similar.

It is a worldwide disorder that you are probably suffering from.

Distraction is robbing you of precious time during the day.

Distraction is robbing you of time that you should be working on your goals.

If you don't rid yourself of distraction, you are in big trouble.

It is a phenomenon that most employees are only productive 3 out of 8 hours at the office.

If you could half your distractions, you could double your productivity.

How far are you willing to go to combat distraction?

How badly do you want to achieve proper time management?

If you know you only have an hour a day to work, would it help keep you focused?

Always focus on your initial reason for doing work in the first place.

After all that reason is still there until you reach your goal.

Create a schedule for your day to keep you from getting distracted.

Distractions are everywhere.

It pops up on your phone.

It pops up from people wanting to chat at work.

It pops up in the form of personal problems.

Whatever it may be, distractions are abound.

The only cure is clear concentration.

To have clear concentration it must be something you are excited about.

To have clear knowledge that this action will lead you to something exciting.

If you find the work boring, It will be difficult for you to concentrate too long.
Sometimes it takes reassessing your life and admitting your work is boring for you to consider a change in direction.

Your goal will have more than one path.
Some paths boring, some paths dangerous, some paths redundant, and some paths magical.
You may not know better until you try.
After all the journey is everything.

If reaching your goal takes decades of work that makes you miserable, is it really worth it?
The changes to your personality may be irreversible.

Always keep the goal in mind whilst searching for an enjoyable path to attain it.
After all if you are easily distracted from your goal, then do you really want it?

Ask yourself the hard questions.
Is this something you really want? Or is this something society wants for you?

Many people who appear successful to society are secretly miserable.
Make sure you are aware of every little detail of your life.
Sit down and really decide what will make you happy at the end of your life.

What work will you be really happy to do?
What are the causes and people you would be happy to serve?
How much money you want?
What kind of relationships you want?
If you can build a clear vision of this life for you, distractions will become irrelevant.
Irrelevant because nothing will be able to distract you from your perfect vision.

Is what you are doing right now moving you towards that life?
If not stop, and start doing the things what will.
It really is that simple.

Anyone who is distracted for too long from the task in hand has no business doing that task. They should instead be doing something that makes them happy.

We can't be happy all the time otherwise we wouldn't be able to recognize it.
But distraction is a clear indicator you may not be on the right path for you.
Clearly define your path and distraction will be powerless.

Chapter 4:

Dealing With Inertia (Gym) Motivation

Inertia, oh dear inertia, if only there was something i can do to make you go away.

Today we are going to talk about why Inertia is so deterimental to anyone's success and how a lack of motivation can prevent you from taking that step forward to your goals. If you don't know already, inertia is a powerful force that pulls you back from doing something that would move the needle in your life, it is like a magnet attracting you and telling you to stay and slack a little more, to lie in bed just a little longer, to keep scrolling Instagram for one more hour because it wouldn't make a difference, or to watch another episode of Netflix while the task just sits on the desk far away from your existence,

Why do I know about inertia so well? Because i struggle with it on a near hourly basis. Inertia knows me so well that it knows exactly what it needs to do or say to keep my staying for one more minute which could turn into hours and before i know it the day is over.

I deal with inertia while trying to get out of bed, get out of the house, and even going to the gym. All these are small but significant personal struggles that rob me of precious time everyday. Inertia battles with my will power on a constant basis that many times it is frankly very difficult to win.

So what can one do to beat inertia to do the things that needs to be done? Sheer determination to win by giving yourself no choice but to get started. You see, inertia can only hold you back for so long, but once you have backed yourself into a corner, you are left with no option but to start. This could mean deleting your Netflix app for just one moment, and turning off wifi, or telling yourself no lunch until you get your ass to the gym. This trick has worked on me time and time again. You see the goal is not to never watch Netflix again, but the act of getting started on your work. For me, once I have tricked my brain into turning the first page, it becomes a lot easier to keep doing the work because my brain doesn't have to keep switching from a mode of relaxation to a mode of working.

You will realise that inertia is like a rubber band, it pulls and pulls but once it snaps, it can't hold u back any longer. And you are free to pursue your day as you see fit. Inertia usually lingers the strongest in the earlier part of the day especially after you have just woken up from bed, but it can also creep up on you at anytime once you have let your guard down and prevented your creative juices from flowing from your powerful brain.

For many of us who have a 9-5 job, inertia is not so much of a problem as you are forced to get up at a specific time of day and to get to office and sit on your desk. And by the time you are at the office 1-2 hours after you have gotten out of bed, the rustiness and inertia would most likely have faded as you are left with no choice but to start your day of work.

Inertia is a 100x greater challenge for those who are entrepreneurs, freelance workers, or those who work from home. Because the freedom to choose your own work schedule means you are not being constantly overlooked by your boss to see if you are actually doing work, and leaving self discipline to yourself can be a dangerous thing with no one to supervise.

With freedom comes responsibility, and without self discipline, one can fall into the trap of easily telling oneself that it is perfectly okay to slack just one more minute. And this can turn into a habit that becomes hard to quit. Inertia is born from habit. And as you know, to break a bad habit one has to also simultaneously form a new healthier and stronger habit that can overpower the other.

So I challenge each and everyone of you to start forming a healthy habit of not procrastinating, of not letting inertia win, and over time, it will have a less and less hold on you anymore until one day you can simply shake it off and start beginning your quest of the day to get you one step closer to your goals.

Chapter 5:

The People You Need in Your Life

We all have friends, the people that are there for us and would be there no matter what. These people don't necessarily need to be different, and these traits might all be in one person. Friends are valuable. You only really ever come across ones that are real. In modern-day society, it's so hard to find friends that want to be your friends rather than just to use you.

Sometimes the few the better, but you need some friends that would guide you along your path. We all need them, and you quite possibly have these traits too. Your friends need you, and you may not even know it.

1. The Mentor

No matter which area or field they are trying to excel in, the common denominator is that they have clarity about life and know exactly what their goals are. These people can impact you tremendously, helps you get into the winners' mindset, infuse self-belief and confidence in you then you, too, can succeed and accomplish your goals. They act as a stepping stone for you to get through your problems. They are happy for your success and would guide you through the troubles and problems while trying to get there.

2. Authentic People

You never feel like you have to make pretense around these people. Life can be challenging enough, so having friends that aren't judging you and are being themselves is very important for your well-being. This type of friend allows you to be vulnerable, express your emotion in healthy ways, and helps bring a smile back to your face when you're down.

They help you also show your true self and how you feel. Rather than showing only a particular side of their personality, they open their whole self to you, allowing you to do the same and feel comfortable around them.

3. Optimists

These people are the kind you need, the ones that will encourage you through tough times. They will be there encouraging you, always seeing the best in the situation. Having the ability to see the best in people and will always have an open mind to situations. Everyone needs optimism in their lives, and these people bring that.

"Optimism is essential to achievement, and it is also the foundation of courage and true progress." -Nicholas M. Butler.

4. Brutally Honest People

To have a balanced view of yourself and be aware of your blind spots is important for you. Be around people who would provide authentic feedback and not sugarcoat while giving an honest opinion about you. They will help you be a better version of yourself, rectifying your mistakes, work on your weak spots, and help you grow. These are the people you can hang around to get better, and you will critique yourself but in a good way, helping you find the best version of yourself. Of course, the ones that are just rude should be avoided, and they should still be nice to you but not too nice to the point where they compliment you even when they shouldn't.

Chapter 6:

Why You Are Setting The Wrong Goals

Ever wondered why you are not getting any closer to your goals? Why you keep failing despite having all that effort? Why does someone else seem to be more successful?

Here are some thoughts for you to ponder.

You may have a good set of skills and all the eligibility criteria anyone else has. But you are not yet in the same spot you wished some years ago. Maybe it is not happening for your right now, because your approach to those goals is not correct. Or, maybe your goals are wrong altogether.

Let's say you had a goal to be someone or achieve something someday. But you never had any idea how to! So you started asking why am I not getting the success that I deserve, but never asked yourself, how can I get to that success.

So you might think that you have the right goals to achieve something. But the reality is, that you never had the right goals.

You should have set a single goal a single day. A single goal that you can achieve in a day will help you get on the right train at the right time with a limited effort.

You shouldn't think of the future itself, but the goal that you might achieve someday. Once you have that goal in mind, you shouldn't need a constant reminder every day just to create a scenario of depression and restlessness that won't help you rather strain unnecessary energy.

Once you have the final goal, put it aside and work towards the small goals that you can achieve in real-time with actual small efforts.

Once you have a grasp of these goals, you will find the next goal yourself; a goal that you might have never thought of before.

Just say you want to lose weight and you want to get to your ideal BMI someday. This is a valid and reasonable Goal to achieve. This might prolong your life and increase your self-worth. So you should have a set of regular goals that ultimately lead you to the final goal.

So you want to lose weight, start by reducing fats and carbs in your next meal, and the one after that and the next one.

It will be hard the first time. Maybe the same at the second time. But when you have envisioned the ultimate goal, you will be content with the healthier alternates as well.

Add 5 minutes of exercise the next day, along with the goals of the previous day. You will be reluctant to do it the first time, but when you see the sweat dripping from your chin, you will see your healthier self in each drop.

Every goal has its process. No matter how much you avoid the process, you will always find yourself at the mercy of mother nature, and nature has always a plan for execution.

Now it's your decision whether to be a part of that process or go down in history with a blank face with no name.

You will always find a way to cheat, but to cheat is another ten steps away from your penultimate goal.

Make it your goal to resist every temptation that makes your day no different than the previous one. Live your life on One day, Monday,

Change day principle and you will always find yourself closer to your salvation.

The process of change is mundane. In fact, the process of everything in life is mundane. You have to apply certain steps and procedures for even doing the most basic tasks in your daily life.

Stop procrastinating because you are not fooling anyone else, just yourself. And if you keep fooling yourself, you will be the worst failure in the books of history.

Chapter 7:

The Power of Developing Eye Contact with Your Client

We've all heard the age-old saying the "eyes are the window to the soul," and in many ways, it holds. Everybody knows looking others in the eyes is beneficial in communication, but how important is eye contact, and how is it defined?

Eye contact can be subtle or even obvious. It can be a glaring scowl when a person is upset or a long glance when we see something off about someone else's appearance. It can even be a direct look when we are trying to express a crucial idea.

1) Respect

In Western countries like the United States, eye contact is critical to show and earn respect. From talking to your boss on the job or thanking your mom for dinner, eye contact shows the other person that you feel equal in importance.

There are other ways to show respect, but our eyes reflect our sincerity, warmth, and honesty.

This is why giving and receiving eye contact while talking is a surefire sign of a good conversation. Nowadays, it's common for people to glance at their phones no matter if they're in the middle of a conversation or not. That's why eye contact will set you apart and truly show that you give them your full and undivided attention.

2) Understanding

Sometimes locking glances is the only sign you need to show someone that you understand what they are talking about. More specifically, if you need to get a vital point across, eye contact is the best way to communicate that importance. Eye contact is also a form of background acknowledgment like saying "yeah" and "mhmm."

That means it shows the speaker that you are tuned in to and understand what they are saying.

3) Bonding

When someone is feeling an emotion or just performing a task, the same neurons that shine in their brain light up in someone else's brain who is watching them. This is because we have "mirror neurons" in our brains that are very sensitive to facial expressions and, most importantly, eye contact.

Direct eye contact is so powerful that it increases empathy and links together emotional states. Never underestimate the power of eye contact in creating long-lasting bonds.

4) Reveal Thoughts and Feelings

We have countless ways of describing eyes, including "shifty-eyed," "kind-eyed," "bright-eyed," "glazed over," and more. It's no wonder just about every classic love story starts with "two pairs of eyes meeting across the room." Eye contact is also a powerful form of simultaneous communication, meaning you don't have to take turns doing the communicating.

Ever wonder why poker players often wear sunglasses inside? It's because "the eyes don't lie." We instinctually look into people's eyes from birth to try and understand what they are thinking, and we continue to do it for life.

Chapter 8:

Don't Fear Judgement

People often seem to get caught up in certain areas of their lives where they have a lot to offer but don't actually have the guts to be transparent about it. Let me make some sense.

We all have this ability to get distracted by things that have very little to do with our actions. But have a lot to do with what others will say about us.

You go through a rough patch in life and then you find the balance. We have things that have been going on in our lives from the beginning, but we still feel doubts about it.

The doubt is natural. But if the doubts are a result of the presence of other people around you, then you have a problem at your hand. This problem is the fear of judgment that everyone imposes on us in their own unique ways.

Humans have a tendency to get out of their ways and try certain things that aren't always normal. They may be normal for some, but for most people out there, it's just another eccentric doing something strange.

So what? What is so bad about being a little different? What is wrong with thinking a little out of the box? Why should your approach be bad if someone doesn't approve of it?

These questions should not make you feel confused. Rather should help you get a much clearer idea of what you want. These questions and their answers can help you find the right motivation. The motivation to do your thing no matter what the others around you say or see.

You are the best judge of your deeds. Because no one else saw your intentions when you started. No one else saw the circumstances that led you to these actions. No other person was in your head looking at and feeling those incidents that carved your present state. But you were always there and always will be.

No one cares what you are up to until you get to the stage of being noticeable. People pass judgments because now you have made it into some sort of limelight. It may be your workplace, your college, or even a party where most people are stoned.

But think about it, what harm can you get with a couple of remarks about your outfit or an achievement?

The words that strike your ears and make you feel incompetent or stupid are just the insecurities of the people around you. The glare of shaming or mockery is only the reflection of the feeling that they don't have what you have.

So be who you are, and say what you want, and do what you feel. Because the people who mind don't matter. But the people who matter would never mind.

Come to terms with yourself and be confident with what you want to do or are currently up to.

No one would understand your reasons and no one is meant to. But they can make a judgment when you are finally on that rostrum. Then you'd have the power to shut anyone at any time.

Chapter 9:
4 Ways to Deal with Feelings of Inferiority When Comparing to Others

When we're feeling inferior, it's usually a result of comparing ourselves to other people and feeling like we don't measure up. And let's be real, it happens all. The. Damn. Time. You could be scrolling through your Instagram feed, notice a new picture of someone you follow, and think: *Wow, how do they always look so perfect?! No amount of filters will make me look like that!* Or maybe you show up to a party, and you quickly realize you're in a room full of accomplished people with exciting lives, and the thought of introducing yourself sends you into a panic. Suddenly, you're glancing at the door and wondering what your best escape plan is. You could be meeting your partner's family for the first time, and you're worried that you won't fit in or that they'll think you're not good enough. You might feel easily intimidated by other people and constantly obsess over what they think of you, even though it's beyond your control.

Don't worry! We have some coping strategies for you that will help you work through your feelings. Try 'em out and see for yourself!

1. Engage in compassionate self-talk

When we feel inferior, we tend to pick ourselves apart and be hard on ourselves. Don't fall into the trap of being your own worst critic! Instead, build your <u>self-confidence</u> and self-esteem by saying positive things to yourself that resonate with you: *I'm feeling inferior right now, but I know my worth. I'm not defined by my credentials, my possessions, or my appearance. I am whole.*

2. Reach out for support or connect with a friend

Just like the Beatles song goes: *I get by with a little help from my friends!* Reach out to someone you can trust and who will be there for you. You might feel inferior now, but it doesn't mean you have to navigate it alone! Get all of those negative feelings off your chest. Having someone there to validate our feelings can be so helpful!

3. Give yourself a pep talk and utilize a helpful statement

Comparing ourselves to other people just brings down our mood and makes us feel like garbage. Sometimes, we gotta give ourselves a little pep talk to turn those negative thoughts around. *I feel inferior right now, but I can get through this! I'm not the only person who has felt this way, and I won't be the last. Everything is gonna be okay!*

4. Comfort yourself like a friend

If you don't have anyone who can be there for you at this moment, that's okay. You can be there for yourself! Think about how you would want a loved one to comfort you at this moment. Pat yourself on the back, treat yourself to some junk food, cuddle up on the couch with a warm, fuzzy blanket and binge your favorite show on Netflix. Be the friend you need right now!

Chapter 10:

Why Are You Working So Hard

Your why,

your reason to get up in the morning,

the reason you act,

really is everything - for without it, there could be nothing.

Your why is the partner of your what,

that is what you want to achieve, your ultimate goal.

Your why will be what pushes you through the hard times on the path to your dreams.

It may be your children or a burning desire to help those less fortunate,

whatever the reason may be,

it is important to keep that in mind when faced with troubles or distractions.

Knowing what you want to do, and why you are doing it,

is of imperative importance for your life.

The tragedy is that most people are aiming for nothing.

They couldn't tell you why they are working in a certain field even if they tried.

Apart from the obvious financial payment,

They have no clue why they are there.

Is financial survival alone really a good motive to act?

Or would financial prosperity be guaranteed if you pursued greater personal preference?

Whatever your ambitions or preference in life,

make sure your why is important enough to you to guarantee your persistence.

Sometimes when pursuing a burning desire,

we can become distracted from the reason we are working.

Your why should be reflected in everything you do.

Once you convince yourself that your reason is important enough, you will not stop.

Despite the hardships, despite the fear, despite the loss and pain.

As long as you maintain a steady path of faith and resilience,

your work will soon start to pay off.

A light will protrude from the darkness and the illusionary troubles sent to test your faith will disappear as if they were never here.

Your why must be strong.

Your what must be as clear as the day is to you now.

And your faith must be eternal and unwavering.

Only then will the doors be opened to you.

This dream can be real, and will be.

When it is clear in the mind with faith, the world will move to show you the way.

The way will be revealed piece by piece, requiring you to take action and do the required work to bring your dream into reality.

Your why is so incredibly important.

The bigger your why, the greater the urgency, and the quicker your action will be.

Take the leap of faith.

Do what you didn't even know you could.

Never mind anyone else.

Taking the unknown path.

Perhaps against the advice of your family and friend,

But you know what your heart wants.

You know that even though the path will be dangerous, the reward will be tremendous.

The risks of not never finding out is too great.

The risk of never knowing if you could have done better is unfathomable.

The Super Man

You can always do better, and you must.

Knowing what is best for you may prove to be the most important thing for you.

How you feel about the work you are doing,

How you feel about the life you are living,

And how do you make the most of the time you have on this earth.

These may prove far more important than financial reward could ever do for you.

Aim to strike a balance.

A balance between working on what you are passionate about and building a wealthy financial life.

If your why and will are strong enough,

Success is all but guaranteed for you – no second guesses needed.

Aim for the sky,

However high you make it,

you will have proven you can indeed fly.

PART 3

Chapter 1:

8 Ways To Love Yourself First

"Your task is not to seek for love, but merely to seek and find all the barriers within yourself that you have built against it." - Rumi.

Most of us are so busy waiting for someone to come into our lives and love us that we have forgotten about the one person we need to love the most – ourselves. Most psychologists agree that being loved and being able to love is crucial to our happiness. As quoted by Sigmund Freud, "love and work ... work and love. That's all there is." It is the mere relationship of us with ourselves that sets the foundation for all other relationships and reveals if we will have a healthy relationship or a toxic one.

Here are some tips on loving yourself first before searching for any kind of love in your life.

1. Know That Self-Love Is Beautiful

Don't ever consider self-love as being narcissistic or selfish, and these are two completely different things. Self-love is rather having positive regard for our wellbeing and happiness. When we adopt self-love, we see higher levels of self-esteem within ourselves, are less critical and harsh with ourselves while making mistakes, and can celebrate our positive qualities and accept all our negative ones.

2. Always be kind to yourself:

We are humans, and humans are tended to get subjected to hurts, shortcomings, and emotional pain. Even if our family, friends, or even our partners may berate us about our inadequacies, we must learn to accept ourselves with all our imperfections and flaws. We look for acceptance from others and be harsh on ourselves if they tend to be cruel or heartless with us. We should always focus on our many positive qualities, strengths, and abilities, and admirable traits; rather than harsh judgments, comparisons, and self-hatred get to us. Always be gentle with yourself.

3. Be the love you feel within yourself:

You may experience both self-love and self-hatred over time. But it would be best if you always tried to focus on self-love more. Try loving yourself and having positive affirmations. Do a love-kindness meditation or spiritual practices to nourish your soul, and it will help you feel love and compassion toward yourself. Try to be in that place of love throughout your day and infuse this love with whatever interaction you have with others.

4. Give yourself a break:

We don't constantly live in a good phase. No one is perfect, including ourselves. It's okay to not be at the top of your game every day, or be happy all the time, or love yourself always, or live without pain. Excuse your bad days and embrace all your imperfections and mistakes. Accept your negative emotions but don't let them overwhelm you. Don't set high standards for yourself, both emotionally and mentally. Don't judge yourself for whatever you feel, and always embrace your emotions wholeheartedly.

5. Embrace yourself:

Are you content to sit all alone because the feelings of anxiety, fear, guilt, or judgment will overwhelm you? Then you have to practice being comfortable in your skin. Go within and seek solace in yourself, practice moments of alone time and observe how you treat yourself. Allow yourself to be mindful of your beliefs, feelings, and thoughts, and embrace solitude. The process of loving yourself starts with understanding your true nature.

6. Be grateful:

Rhonda Bryne, the author of The Magic, advises, "When you are grateful for the things you have, no matter how small they may be, you will see those things instantly increase." Look around you and see all the things that you are blessed to have. Practice gratitude daily and be thankful for all the things, no matter how good or bad they are. You will immediately start loving yourself once you realize how much you have to be grateful for.

7. Be helpful to those around you:

You open the door for divine love the moment you decide to be kind and compassionate toward others. "I slept and dreamt that life was a joy. I awoke and saw that life was service. I acted, and behold, and service was a joy." - Rabindranath Tagore. The love and positive vibes that you wish upon others and send out to others will always find a way back to you. Your soul tends to rejoice when you are kind, considerate, and compassionate. You have achieved the highest form of self-love when you decide to serve others. By helping others, you will realize that you don't need someone else to feel complete; you are complete. It will help you feel more love and fulfillment in your life.

8. Do things you enjoy doing:

If you find yourself stuck in a monotonous loop, try to get some time out for yourself and do the things that you love. There must be a lot of hobbies and passions that you might have put a brake on. Dust them off and start doing them again. Whether it's playing any sport, learning a new skill, reading a new book, writing in on your journal, or simply cooking or baking for yourself, start doing it again. We shouldn't compromise on the things that make us feel alive. Doing the things we enjoy always makes us feel better about ourselves and boost our confidence.

Conclusion:

Loving yourself is nothing short of a challenge. It is crucial for your emotional health and ability to reach your best potential. But the good news is, we all have it within us to believe in ourselves and live the best life we possibly can. Find what you are passionate about, appreciate yourself, and be grateful for what's in your life. Accept yourself as it is.

Chapter 2:

8 Ways to Discover What's holding You Back From Achieving Your Visions

We all have dreams, and I have no questions; you have made attempts at seeking after your goals. Oh, as a general rule, life's battles get the better of you and keep you down. The pressure of everyday life, again and again, puts you down. Regardless of your determination, devotion, and want, alone, they are not enough.

Being here exhibits you are not able to settle for a mediocre life and hidden desires. To help you in your goal of seeking after your objectives, you must become acquainted with those things keeping you down. When you do, you will want to eliminate every single reason keeping you down.

1. Fear

The deep-rooted foe is very likely a critical factor in keeping many of you from seeking after your objectives. It prevents you from acting, making you scared of venturing out. Dread is the thing that keeps you down. Dread is one reason why we don't follow what we truly need throughout everyday life.

- Fear of disappointment
- Fear of dismissal
- Fear of mocking

• Fear of disappointment

Quit allowing your feelings of fear to keep you down!

2. Procrastination

Putting things off till the following week, one month from now, one year from now, and regularly forever. You're not exactly sure the thing you're hanging tight for, but rather when whatever it happens, you'll be prepared to start seeking after your objectives. Be that as it may, this day never comes. Your fantasy stays as just a fantasy. Putting things off can just keep you down.

Quit allowing your Procrastination to keep you down!

3. Justifications

Do you find yourself procrastinating and making excuses for why you can't start working toward your goals? Those that succeed in accomplishing their objectives can overcome obstacles. So many individuals make excuses for themselves, believing they can't achieve a better career, start their own business, or find their ideal lifemate.

• It isn't the correct time

• I am insufficient

• I am too old/young

Don't allow your excuses to hold you back any longer!

4. Lack of Confidence

Lack of confidence in yourself or your ability to achieve your goals will inevitably hold you back. Our actions, or lack thereof, are influenced by what goes on in our subconscious mind. We have self-limiting and negative beliefs that may be preventing us from enjoying an extraordinary life.

Nothing will be able to stop you if you believe in yourself. Bringing your limiting beliefs into focus will help you achieve your objectives.

Don't let your lack of confidence keep you back!

5. There Isn't A Big Picture

Others refer to what I call a breakthrough goal as a BHAG - Big Hairy Audacious Goal. A goal is what you need to keep you motivated and drive you to achieve it every day. Start small and dream big. You'll need a strong enough passion to propel you forward. Your ambitions will not motivate you until you first dream big.

For your objectives to be beneficial to you, they must assist you in realizing your ambitions. Those lofty ambitions. Goals can only motivate you, help you stay focused, and help you make the adjustments you need to make, as well as provide you the fortitude to overcome difficulties as you chase your big-picture dreams if they matter to you.

Stop allowing your big picture to stifle your progress!

6. Inability To Concentrate

Your chances of success are slashed every moment you lose focus. When we spread our focus too thin, we dilute our effort and lose the ability to focus on the most significant tasks. When you're pulled in a lot of different directions and have a lot of conflicting priorities fighting for your attention, it's easy to lose track of what's important. Any attempts to achieve vital goals will be harmed as a result of this.

Stop allowing your lack of concentration to keep you back!

7. Failure to Make a Plan

Finally, if you don't have a strategy, it's easy to become lost along the route. Consider driving across the country without a map, say from London to Glasgow. While you have a rough route in mind, there are many lands to cover and a lot of false turns and dead ends to be avoided. You can get there with the help of a GPS. It plots your path and creates a plan for you. A plan provides you with the road map you need to reach your objectives. This is the process of determining what you need to accomplish to reach your objectives. This is where you put in the time and effort to write out a plan of the steps you need to follow, the resources you'll need, and the amount of time you'll need to invest.

Stop allowing the lack of a strategy holds you back!

8. Not Keeping Track of Your Progress and Making Necessary Modifications

Goals, by their very nature, take time to attain. Therefore it's critical to keep track of your progress. You won't know what's working and what's not if you don't get quick and actionable feedback. You won't be able to tell when to alter or when to keep doing what you're doing. Anyone who is continuously successful in accomplishing their goals also reviews their goals and progress regularly. Regularly reviewing your goals allows you to make early modifications to stay on track.

Stop allowing not reviewing and adjusting your progress to hold you back!

Chapter 3:

6 Steps To Get Out of Your Comfort Zone

The year 2020 and 2021 have made a drastic change in all our lives, which might have its effect forever. The conditions of last year and a half have made a certain lifestyle choice for everyone, without having a say in it for us.

This new lifestyle has been a bit overwhelming for some and some started feeling lucky. Most of us feel comfortable working from home, and taking online classes while others want to have some access to public places like parks and restaurants.

But the pandemic has affected everyone more than once. And now we are all getting used to this relatively new experience of doing everything from home. Getting up every day to the same routine and the same environment sometimes takes us way back on our physical and mental development and creativity.

So one must learn to leave the comfort zone and keep themselves proactive. Here are some ways anyone can become more productive and efficient.

Everyone is always getting ready to change but never changing.

1. Remember your Teenage Self

People often feel nostalgic remembering those days of carelessness when they were kids and so oblivious in that teenage. But, little do they take for inspiration or motivation from those times. When you feel down, or when you don't feel like having the energy for something, just consider your teenage self at that time.

If only you were a teenager now, you won't be feeling lethargic or less motivated. Rather you'd be pushing harder and harder every second to get the job done as quickly as possible. If you could do it back then, you still can! All you need is some perspective and a medium to compare to.

2. Delegate or Mentor someone

Have you ever needed to have someone who could provide you some guidance or help with a problem that you have had for some time?

I'm sure, you weren't always a self-made man or a woman. Somewhere along the way, there was someone who gave you the golden quote that changed you consciously or subconsciously.

Now is the time for you to do the same for someone else. You could be a teacher, a speaker, or even a mentor who doesn't have any favors to ask in return. Once you get the real taste of soothing someone else's pain, you won't hesitate the next time.

This feeling of righteousness creates a chain reaction that always pushes you to get up and do good for anyone who could need you.

3. Volunteer in groups

The work of volunteering may seem pointless or philanthropic. But the purpose for you to do it should be the respect that you might get, but the stride to get up on your feet and help others to be better off.

Volunteering for flood victims, earthquake affectees or the starving people of deserts and alpines can help you understand the better purpose of your existence. This keeps the engine of life running.

4. Try New Things for a Change

Remember the time in Pre-school when your teachers got you to try drawing, singing, acting, sculpting, sketching, and costume parties. Those weren't some childish approach to keep you engaged, but a planned system to get your real talents and skills to come out.

We are never too old to learn something new. Our passions are unlimited just as our dreams are. We only need a push to keep discovering the new horizons of our creative selves.

New things lead to new people who lead to new places which might lead to new possibilities. This is the circle of life and life is ironic enough to rarely repeat the same thing again.

You never know which stone might lead you to a gold mine. So never stop discovering and experiencing because this is what makes us the supreme being.

5. Push Your Physical Limits

This may sound cliched, but it always is the most important point of them all. You can never get out of your comfort zone, till you see the world through the hard glass.

The world is always softer on one side, but the image on the other side is far from reality. You can't expect to get paid equally to the person who works 12 hours a day in a large office of hundreds of employees. Only if you have the luxury of being the boss of the office.

You must push yourself to search for opportunities at every corner. Life has always more and better to offer at each stop, you just have to choose a stop.

6. Face Your Fears Once and For All

People seem to have a list of Dos and Dont's. The latter part is mostly because of a fear or a vacant thought that it might lead to failure for several reasons.

You need a "Do it all" behavior in life to have an optimistic approach to everything that comes in your way.

What is the biggest most horrible thing that can happen if you do any one of these things on your list? You need to have a clear vision of the possible worst outcome.

If you have a clear image of what you might lose, now must try to go for that thing and remove your fear once and for all. Unless you have something as important as your life to lose, you have nothing to fear from anything.

No one can force you to directly go skydiving if you are scared of heights. But you can start with baby steps, and then, maybe, later on in life you dare to take a leap of faith.

"Life is a rainbow, you might like one color and hate the other. But that doesn't make it ugly, only less tempting".

All you need is to be patient and content with what you have today, here, right now. But, you should never stop aiming for more. And you certainly shouldn't regret it if you can't have or don't have it now.

People try to find their week spots and frown upon those moments of hard luck. What they don't realize is, that the time they wasted crying for what is in the past, could have been well spent for a far better future they could cherish for generations to come.

Chapter 4:

7 Ways To Develop Effective Communication With Your Clients

Effective communication is a significant factor in business; it is the essence of your business as clients are the core of every business. Sometimes, we forget what the client wanted; if this has happened to you, then you that your communication skills need a tad bit of improvement. The relationships you build with your clients are the key. Gaining loyal customers is essential, as they buy from you repeatedly and refer you to others, which increases customers. Communication can take many shapes and forms; it can be formal or informal and can happen over various platforms. Here are seven ways to develop practical communication skills with your clients.

1. Make It About Your Clients

When you meet someone that requires your services, you need to make it about them. It would help if you indeed gained your client's trust, but that doesn't mean the client has to hear your whole life story or several awards you have won. So whenever a new client seeks out help, remember that it is them that need help and focus on how you can impress them and meet their requirements. It is the best way to demonstrate your experience and extensive knowledge about the subject.

2. Treat Them How You'd Like To Be Treated

Business can be very tiring, sometimes when the stress is overbearing, we might feel moody and irritated but try not to take out the irritation on the clients, as your business exists because of your clients, so being rude with them will not be very wise. Try to be more patient, friendly, and positive with them, and your positive behavior shows your eagerness for your work. So try to treat your customers the most excellent way possible, the way you would want to be treated.

3. Respect Your Client's Time

"Time is money" we all have heard this famous saying, but what does it mean? The sentence gives away its meaning. It means that time is precious, whether it's yours or your clients'. Hence, try to avoid talking too much or wasting their time. Try not to make them wait for you too much that may cause unhealthiness in your relationship with your client. Try to get to the point without sounding rude or being blunt, be concise. Over media platforms, a short and well-planned consultation probably will do the work, and if they need any more information, they would ask you.

4. Listen To Your Clients

We all have met that annoying salesman that doesn't understand what you want or doesn't let you finish. If you have met someone like that, you know how irritating it could be, so when it is your time to be a businessman, don't do the same. When talking to your clients, please give them your undivided attention; you could do that by clearing up your brain of everything, no matter how busy the day is and how long the to-do list is. Take notes if you think you need them; try not to interrupt and stay silent if you think the customer wants to add a few more points. Listen actively to the client so that you can provide better customer service.

5. Pay Attention To What Your Clients Say

Any relationship requires attention; without attention, a client may seem very happy, and your business might not flourish the way you want it to. So pay attention to the tiniest of details of what the clients say. Take notes of the information that is hard to remember or seems essential. Ensure that you respond to emails, requests, or questions about your business; it will make the clients feel important. When sending out an email to your clients, double-check and see if you had made any mistakes, grammar mistakes indicate carelessness, and what kind of a client would want a careless person to help them.

6. Actively Build Your Client Communication Skills

If you want to create a lasting relationship with your customers, focus on your communication skills; you could set up a few rules and principles for yourself and your team to follow—brief your team on how to be friendly and provide the customer service required by the client. You can ask your client for their feedback on customer service; if they share something they don't like, you and your team can together work on that. Also, use client communication tools and software.

7. Keep Records of Your Interactions

Always keep records of your previous conversations with your clients; if you forgot a minor detail that was not so minor for them, it might not end pleasantly. Even the people who give clients their undivided attention forget things. So you could keep records of your interactions with your clients by making notes on a file or your mobile phone or by recording the conversation after they allow you. Making notes will also help you later, as it will help you remember who you need to check up on or follow up with.

Conclusion

Try to follow these ways, and win the trust of your clients. Be friendly and pleasant, and your clients will stay happy with you.

Chapter 5:

6 Ways to Start All Over Again

If anyone tells you that you're meant to go from the crib to the running track, breeze through college, get your dream job, score the perfect partner, and live happily ever after all in one fell swoop, they're lying…and seriously delusional.

The reality is that life is anything but a straight line and is made up of seasons — some good, some mundane, and some so bad that you'll need plenty of time to recover from the trauma of living through it.

At your lowest point, you may think that your life is ruined and there's no way out.

But *listen* to me: **It WILL pass.** There's *always* a way forward. You just have to look for it. You can let the circumstances you're in ruin you, or you can allow it to improve you.

The process of rebuilding your life from the ground up won't be easy, but having a plan will greatly increase your chances of successfully carving out the life you want.

Here are my tried-and-tested steps to start with:

1. Start With Cleaning Up the Space You Live In

To build something good, you'll need good daily habits.

But to turn a new, unfamiliar (and therefore uncomfortable and 'quit-able') action into a daily habit, you'll need to do everything you can to reduce the odds that you'll give up, particularly when you hit a speed bump.

One of the best ways to do this is to set up your environment for your success.

This means clearing the space where you spend the most time of clutter, trash, and chaos.

The result: A calmer, clearer, and focused mind that'll help you move forward with your plan and sticking to it.

2. Make Peace With Reality and Work With, Not Against It

We often get stuck in life because we're either unable or unwilling to accept our reality as it is. Instead, we stubbornly continue to indulge in fantasy, specifically, how we wish things were.

This is where you'll need to get real with yourself, no matter how unpleasant it is.

Ask yourself: What's your situation now, and how can you work with what is, not what you wish it was?

3. Reflect On What and Where You Went Wrong

No one starts out planning to fail or creating a disaster.

But somehow, we end up taking one or several wrong steps along the way and find ourselves on a painful path we never expected to be in.

Whether these missteps were driven by ego, a lack of awareness, miscalculation, denial, or simply carelessness, you owe it to yourself, to be honest with the captain of your ship: You.

It's only once you've taken the time to reflect and figure out what went wrong and where things started to fall apart that you can start putting together a new plan with your success-driving strategy baked in.

This is the plan that'll help you make the progress you've wanted all along.

4. Revisit Your Goals and Values

But wait.

Before you take one step forward on your new path, you'll need to make sure your foundation is solid.

You may have an idea of where you'd like to go: Run it through a stress test:

How do you want to live?

Does your idea align with your values?

What are your values anyway?

What will you do if someone close to you disagrees or tries to tear it down?

What will happen if you find yourself feeling tempted to stray away from it?

Put your ideas, values, and stress-test answers down on paper so you can see them all in one place and let them sink in.

5. Decide what you Want To Do Next

Now that you've some ideas for possible paths you could take that fall in line with your values, it's time to decide: Which one will you choose?

'Decision' comes from the Latin word decision, which means "to cut off."

But while picking one path means cutting yourself off from all others, it doesn't mean that you can't course-correct later on by choosing a different one if things don't work out or feel right.

6. Work Up The Courage To Do It

It's OK to feel terrified about heading into new, unchartered territory. It'd be weird if you didn't. But know that this is the point where you start putting one foot in front of the other regardless of how you feel or chicken out and retreat into your cave. It's time to get moving despite the paralyzing fear and soul-crushing doubt that are making your feet and heart feel like lead.

Chapter 6:

6 Ways On How To Change Your Body Language To Attract Success

"If you want to find the truth, do not listen to the words coming to you. Rather see the body language of the speaker. It speaks the facts not audible." - Bhavesh Chhatbar.

Our body language is exceptionally essential as 60-90% of our communication with others is nonverbal. If properly used, it can be our key to more tremendous success. We focus more on our business plans, our marketing drives, and our spreadsheets rather than considering our facial expressions, posture, or what our physical gestures might be saying about us. Our mindset also plays a role in how our body language expresses itself. No matter how impressive our words maybe, if we are sending a negative signal with our body language, we would eventually lose the opportunities of gaining more success.

Here is a list to help you change your body language to attract more success.

1. The Power of Voice

Your personal voice has a huge impact and can literally make or break your success. It is one of the most direct routes to empower your communication. The pitch of your voice, its timbre, cadence, volume, and the speed with which you speak, are all influential factors that will ensure how convincing you are and how people will judge your character. Lowering your voice at the right moment or injecting some spontaneity into it when needed will enhance your credibility and lend you an air of intelligence. We must fill our voices with our range and depth if we want others and ourselves to take us seriously.

2. The Power of Listening

An excellent speaking skill represents only half of the leadership expression. The other half is mastering your art in listening. While a good listener is incredibly rare, it is essential to keep our ears open to any valuable information that is often silently transmitted. When we start listening attentively to others, we begin to notice what a person is saying and decode accurately what they don't say. You will also begin to realize what the other person is thinking or whether their attitude is positive or hostile towards you. With these particular observations, you will likely attune to another person and create the bond crucial to a successful working life.

3. The Necessity for Emotional Intelligence

The skill of acute listening develops our emotional intelligence, the intuition to ascertain the objective reality of the situation. When we lack emotional intelligence, we might misinterpret situations and fail to decipher what might be needed. Emotional intelligence deepens our empathy. It gives us the ability to be present and listen to someone when they need it the most. It is the single best predictor of performance in the workplace and can be the most vital driver of personal excellence and leadership. Our understanding of emotional intelligence will vastly improve our internal relations and can also deepen our sense of personal fulfillment and professional accomplishment.

4. The Power of Eye Contact

Making eye contact and holding it is seen as a sign of confidence, and the other person is felt valued. It increases your chance of being trustful and respected as they tend to listen to you more attentively and feel comfortable giving you their insights. You may be shy, an introvert, or might have heard that it's impolite to maintain eye contact with a superior. But in many parts of the world, business people expect you to maintain eye contact 50-60% of the time. Here's a simple tip: when you meet someone, look into their eyes long enough to notice their eye color.

5. Talk With Your Hands

There's a region in our brain called the Broca's area, which is essential and active during our speech production and when we wave our hands. Gestures are integrally linked to speech, so gesturing while talking can speed up your thinking. Using hand gestures while talking can improve verbal content as well as make your speechless hesitant. You will see that it will help you form clearer thoughts with more declarative language and speak in tighter sentences.

6. Strike A Power Pose

Research conducted at Harvard and Columbia Business Schools into the effects of body posture and confidence show that holding your body in expansive high-power poses (such as leaning back with hands behind the head or standing with legs and arms stretched wide open) for only as little as two minutes can stimulate high levels of testosterone (a hormone linked to power) and lower levels of cortisol (a stress hormone). You will look and feel more confident and inevitable, leading to an increased feeling of energy and a high tolerance for risk.

Conclusion

Most of our body language and movement are subconscious, so it can be challenging to retrain ourselves away from habits we have had for years. Still, we must try to master our body language, too, with the art of public speaking. Regular practice Is the key to success and the quickest route to attain confident body language as with any other skill. Practice them in your day-to-day life so that they may become deep-rooted. Be less compliant and step into an edgier, emboldened, and more genuine you.

Chapter 7:

5 Ways To Adopt Right Attitude For Success

Being successful is a few elements that require hard work, dedication, and a positive attitude. It requires building your resilience and having a clear idea of your future ahead. Though it might be hard to decide your life forward, a reasonable manner is something that comes naturally to those who are willing to give their all. Adopting a new attitude doesn't always mean to change yourself in a way but, it has more meaning towards changing your mindset to an instinct. That is when you get stressed or overworked is because of an opposing point of view on life.

With success comes a great sense of dealing with things. You become more professional, and you feel the need to achieve more in every aspect. Don't be afraid to be power-hungry. But, it also doesn't mean to be unfair. Try to go for a little more than before, each step ahead. Make your hard work or talent count in every aspect. Make yourself a successful person in a positive manner, so you'll find yourself making the most of yourself. And don't give up on the things you need in life.

1. Generate Pragmatic Impressions

"The first impression is the last impression." It's true that once you've introduced yourself to the person in front of you, there is only a tiny chance that you'll get to introduce yourself again. So, choosing the correct wording while creating an impression is a must. You need to be optimistic about yourself and inform the other person about you in a way that influences them. An impression that leaves an effect on them, so they will willingly meet you again. A person must be kind and helpful towards its inferior and respectful towards their superior. This is one of the main characteristics for a person to be a successful man or woman. And with a negative attitude, the opposite occurs. People are more inclined to work without you. They nearly never consider you to work with them and try to contact you as little as possible. So, a good impression is significant.

2. Be True To Your Words

Choose your wording very carefully, because once said, it can't be taken back. Also, for a successful life, commitment is always an important rule. Be true to what you said to a person. Make them believe that they can trust you comfortably. So, it would be best if you chose your words. Don't commit if you can't perform. False commitment leads to loss of customers and leads to the loss of your impression as a successful worker. Always make sure that you fulfill your commands and promises to your clients and make them satisfied with your performance. It leads to a positive mindset and a dedication to work towards your goal.

3. A Positive Personal Life

Whatever you may be doing in your professional life can impact your personal life too. Creating the right mindset professionally also helps you to keep a positive attitude at home. It allows you to go forward with the proper consultation with your heart. It will make you happier. You'll desire to achieve more in life because you'll be satisfied with your success. It will push to go furthermore. It will drive you towards the passion for desiring more. Hard work and determination will continue to be your support, and you will be content will your heart. By keeping a good attitude, you'll be helping yourself more than helping others.

4. Be Aggressive and Determined

Becoming goal-oriented is one of the main factors evolving success in your life. If you are not determined to do your work, you'll just accept things the way others present you. It will leave you in misery and deeply dissatisfied with yourself. Similarly, you'll tend to do something more your way if you are goal-oriented and not how others want. You'll want to shale everything according to your need, and you become delighted with yourself and the result of your hard work. Always keep a clear view of your next step as it will form you in to your true self. Don't just go with the flow, but try to change it according to your wants and needs.

5. Create Your Master Plan

Indeed, we can't achieve great things with only hard work. We will always need to add a factor or to in our business. But by imagining or strategizing, some plans might be helpful. With hard work and some solid projects, we will get our desired outcome. If not, at least we get something close. And if you chose the wrong option, then the amount of hard work won't matter. You'll never get what you want no matter the hard work. So, always make sure to make plans strategically.

Conclusion

By keeping a positive attitude, you'll not only be helpful to others but to yourself too. Make sure you keep the proper manner—a manner required to be a successful person. Do lots of achievements and try to prove yourself as much as possible. Try keeping a good impact on people around you in everything you do. Have the spirit and courage to achieve great heights. And be sure to make moat of yourself. Consistency is the key.

Chapter 8:

5 Lessons on Being Wrong

Being wrong isn't as bad as we make it out to be. I have made many mistakes, and I have discovered five major lessons from my experiences.

1. Choices that seem poor in hindsight are an indication of growth, not self-worth or intelligence. When you look back on your choices from a year ago, you should always hope to find a few decisions that seem stupid now because that means you are growing. If you only live in the safety zone where you know you can't mess up, then you'll never unleash your true potential. If you know enough about something to make the optimal decision on the first try, then you're not challenging yourself.

2. Given that your first choice is likely to be wrong, the best thing you can do is get started. The faster you learn from being wrong, the sooner you can discover what is right. Complex situations like relationships or entrepreneurship have to start before you feel ready because no one can be truly ready. The best way to learn is to start practicing.

3. Break down topics that are too big to master into smaller tasks that can be mastered. I can't look at any business and tell you what to do. Entrepreneurship is too big of a topic. But, I can look at any website and tell you how to optimize it for building an email list because that topic is small enough for me to develop some level of expertise. If you want to get better at making accurate first choices, then play in a smaller arena. As Niels Bohr, the Nobel Prize-winning physicist, famously said, "An expert is a person who has made all the mistakes that can be made in a very narrow field."

4. The time to trust your gut is when you have the knowledge or experience to back it up. You can trust yourself to make sharp decisions in areas where you already have proven expertise. For everything else, the only way to discover what works is to adopt a philosophy of experimentation.

5. The fact that failure will happen is not an excuse for expecting to fail. There is no reason to be depressed or give up simply because you will make a few wrong choices. Even more crucial, you must try your best every time because the effort and the practice drive the learning process. They are essential, even if you fail. Realize that no single choice is destined to fail, but that occasional failure is <u>the cost you must pay if you want to be right</u>. Expect to win and play like it from the outset.

Your first choice is rarely the optimal choice. Make it now, <u>stop judging yourself</u>, and start growing.

Achieving Happiness

Happiness is a topic that is at the core of this channel. Because as humans we all want to be happy in some way shape or form. Happiness strikes as something that we all want to strive for because how can we imagine living an unhappy life. It might be possible but it wouldn't be all that fun no matter how you spin it. However I'm gonna offer another perspective that would challenge the notion of happiness and one that maybe would be more attainable for the vast majority of people.

So why do we as humans search for happiness? It is partly due to the fact that it has been ingrained in us since young that we all should strive to live a happy and healthy life. Happiness has become synonymous with the very nature of existence that when we find ourselves unhappy in any given moment, we tend to want to pivot our life and the current situation we are in to one that is more favourable, one that is supposedly able to bring us more happiness.

But how many of us are actually always happy all the time? I would argue that happiness is not at all sustainable if we were feeling it at full blast constantly. After a while we would find ourselves being numb to it and maybe that happiness would turn into neutrality or even boredom. There were times in my life where i felt truly happy and free. I felt that i had great friends around me, life had limitless possibilities, the weather was great, the housing situation was great, and i never wanted it to end as i knew that it was the best time of my life.

However knowing that this circumstance is only temporary allowed me to cherish each and every moment more meaningfully. As i was aware that time was not infinite and that some day this very state of happiness would somehow end one way or another, that i would use that time wisely and spend them with purpose and meaning. And it was this sense that nothing ever lasts forever that helped me gain a new perspective on everything i was doing at that present moment in time. Of course, those happy times were also filled with times of trials, conflicts, and challenges, and they made that period of my life all the more memorable and noteworthy.

For me, happiness is a temporary state that does not last forever. We might be happy today but sad tomorrow, but that is perfectly okay and totally fine. Being happy all the time is not realistic no matter how you spin it. The excitement of getting a new house and new car would soon fade from the moment you start driving in it, and that happiness you once thought you associated with it can disappear very quickly. And that is okay. Because life is about constant change and nothing really ever stays the same.

With happiness comes with it a whole host of different emotions that aims to highlight and enhance its feeling. Without sadness and sorrow, happiness would have no counter to be matched against. It is like a yin without a yang. And we need both in order to survive.

I believe that to be truly happy, one has to accept that sadness and feelings of unhappiness will come as a package deal. That whilst we want to be happy, we must also want to feel periods of lull to make the experience more rewarding.

I challenge all of you today to view happiness as not something that is static and that once you achieved it that all will be well and life will be good, but rather a temporary state of feeling that will come again and again when you take steps to seek it.

I also want to bring forth to you an alternative notion to happiness, in the form of contentment, that we will discuss in the next video. Take care and I'll see you there.

Chapter 9:

Five Steps to Clarify Your Goals

Today, we're going to talk about how and why you should start clarifying your goals. But first, let me ask you, why do you think setting clear goals is important?

Well, imagine yourself running at a really fast speed, but you don't know where you're going. You just keep running and running towards any direction without a destination in mind. What do you think will happen next? You'll be exhausted. But will you feel fulfilled? Not really. Why? Because despite running at breakneck speed and being busy, you have failed to identify an end point. Without it, you won't know how far or near you are to where you are supposed to be. The same analogy applies to how we live our lives. No matter how productive you are or how fast your pacing is, at the end the race, if you don't have clear goals, you will simply end up wondering what the whole point of running was in the first place. You might end up in a place that you didn't intend to be. Neglecting the things that are most important on you, while focusing on all the wrong things- and that is not the best way to live your life.

So, how can we change that? How can we clarify our goals so that we are sure that we are running the race we intended to all along?

1.   Imagine The Ideal Version of Yourself

Try to picture the kind of person you want to be. The things you want to have. The people you want around you. The kind of life that your ideal self is living. How does your ideal-self make small and big decisions? How does he or she perceive the world? Don't limit your imagination to what you think is pleasant and acceptable in society.

Fully integrate that ideal image of yourself into your subconscious mind and see yourself filling those shoes. That is the only way that you'll be able to see it as a real person.

Remember that the best version of yourself doesn't need to be perfect. But this is your future life so dream as big as you want, and genuinely believe that you'll be able to become that person someday in the near future.

2. Identify The Gap Between Your Ideal and Present Self

Take a hard look at your current situation now and ask yourself honesty: "How far am I away now from the person I know I need to become one day? What am I lacking at present that I am not doing or acting upon? Are there any areas that I can identify that I need to work on? Are there any new habits that I need to adopt to become that person?

Be unbiased in your self-assessment as that is the only way to give yourself a clear view of knowing exactly what you need to start working on today. Be brutally honest with your self-evaluation.

It is okay to be starting from scratch if that is where are at this point. Don't be afraid of the challenge, instead embrace and prepare yourself for the journey of a lifetime. It is way worse not knowing when and where to begin than starting from nothing at all.

3. Start Making Your Action Plan

Once you have successfully identified the gap between your present self and your ideal self, start to list down all the actions you need to take and the things that need to be done. Breakdown your action plan into milestones. Make it specific, measurable and realistic. If your action plans don't work the way you think they will, don't be afraid to make new plans. Remember that your failed plans are just part of the whole journey so enjoy every moment of it. Don't be hard on yourself while you're in the process. You're a human and not a machine. Don't forget to rest and recharge from time to time. You will be more inspired and will have more energy to go through your action plan if you are taking care of yourself at the same time.

4.   Set A Timeline

Now that you have identified your overarching goal and objectives, set a period of time when you think it is reasonable for a certain milestone to be completed. You don't need to be so rigid with this timeline. Instead use it as sort of a guiding light. This guide is to serve as a reminder to provide a sense of urgency to work on your goals consistently. Don't beat yourself up unnecessarily if you do not meet your milestones as you have set up. Things change and problems do come up in our lives. As long as you keep going, you're perfectly fine. Remember that it is not about how slow or how fast you get to your destination, it is about how you persevere to continue your journey.

5.   Aim For Progress, Not Perfection

You are living in an imperfect world with an imperfect system. Things will never be perfect but it doesn't mean that it will be less beautiful. While you're in the process of making new goals and working on them as you go along, always make room for mistakes and adjustments. You can plan as much as you want but life has its own way of doing things. When unforeseen events take place, don't be afraid to make changes and adjustments, or start over if you must. Even though things will not always go the way you want them to, you can still be in control of choosing how you'll move forward.

As humans, we never want to be stuck. We always want to be somewhere better. But sometimes, we get lost along the way. If we have a clear picture of where we want to be, no matter how many detours we encounter, we'll always find our way to get to our destination. And you know what, sometimes those detours are what we exactly need to keep going through our journey.

Chapter 10:

Consistency Can Bring You Happiness

Happiness is an individual concept.

One man's riches is another man's rubbish.

As humans we are not happy if we do not have a routine, a reason to get up, and a purpose to live.

Without working towards something consistently, we become lost.

We begin to drift.

Drifting with no purpose eventually leads to emptiness.

When we are drifting in a job we hate,

We are trading our future away,

When we inconsistent in our relationships,

Problems are bound to arise.

Choose consistent focus instead.

Figure out exactly what you want and start to change it.

Employ consistent routines and habits that to move you towards your goals.

Consistency and persistence are key to success and happiness.

Without consistent disciplined effort towards what we want, we resign to a life of mediocrity.

Read a book for an hour consistently every single day.

You will become a national expert in 1 year.

In 5 years, a global expert.

That is the power of consistency.

Instead, people spend most of their free time scrolling through social media.

Consistency starts in the mind.

Control your thoughts to be positive despite the circumstances.

Nothing in the world can make us happy if we choose not to be.

Choose to be happy now and consistently working towards your goals.

We cannot be happy and successful if we dwell in the day to day setbacks.

We must consistently move like a bulldozer.

We have to keep going no matter what.

Nothing stays in the path of a bulldozer for too long.

In life, no matter where you are, you only ever have two choices.

Choose to stay where you are? Or choose to keep moving?

If where you are is making you happy, then by all means do more of it.

If not. What will? And why?

This should be clear before you take action.

Start with the end in your mind.

Let your body catch-up to it afterwards.

The end result is your what.

The action required is your how.

Concentrate on the what and the how and it will all be revealed soon enough.

Concentrate consistently on what you want for yourself and your family.

Distraction and lack of consistent action is a killer of happiness and success.

Your happiness is the life you want.

Take consistent action towards that life you've always dreamed of.

Commitment and endurance is part of that process.

On earth things need time to nurture and grow.

Everything in life depends on it.

The right conditions for maximum growth.

You can't just throw a seed on the concrete and expect it to grow with no soil and water,

Just as you can't simply wish for change and not create the right environment for success.

A seed requires not just consistent sunlight,

But the perfect combination of water and nutrients as well.

You might have given that seed sunlight,

just as you have your dream hope,

But without faith and consistent action towards the goal, nothing will happen.

The seed will still stay a seed forever.

Consistency in thought and action is everything towards happiness.

Nothing can grow without it.

Your success can be measured by your time spent working towards your goals.

If we consistently do nothing we become successful in nothing.

If we have to do something, should it not be something worth doing?

Start doing things that make you happy and fulfilled.

Consistency towards something that makes you happy is key towards lasting success.

Adapt when necessary but remain consistent with the end result in mind.

The path can be changed when necessary but the destination cannot.

Accepting anything less is admitting defeat.

Consistent concentration on the end result can and will be tested.

It however cannot be defeated, unless you quit.

If we remain steadfast in our belief that this is possible for us, it will be possible.

After a while things will seem probable. Eventually it becomes definite.

Continue to believe you can do it despite the circumstances.

Continue despite everyone around you saying you can't do it.

In spite of social status,
in spite of illness or disability,
in spite of age, race or nationality,
know you can do nearly anything if you consistently put all of your mind and body
towards the task.

Take the pressure off.
There is no set guideline.
It is what you make of it.

There is no set destination or requirements.
Those are set my you.

The only competition is yourself from yesterday.
If you can consistently outperform that person, your success is guaranteed.
Consistent concentration and action towards your dream is key you your success and
happiness.

7 Ways To Cultivate Emotions That Will Lead You To Greatness

Billions of men and women have walked the earth but only a handful have made their names engraved in history forever. These handful of people have achieved 'greatness' owing to their outstanding work, their passion and their character.

Now, greatness doesn't come overnight—greatness is not something you can just reach out and grab. Greatness is the result of how you have lived your entire life and what you have achieved in your lifetime. Against all your given circumstances, how impactful your life has been in this world, how much value you have given to the people around you, how much difference your presence has made in history counts towards how great you are. However, even though human greatness is subjective, people who are different and who have stood out from everyone else in a particular matter are perceived as great.

However, cultivating greatness in life asks for a 'great' deal of effort and all kinds of human effort are influenced by human emotions. So it's safe to say that greatness is, in fact, controlled by our emotions. Having said that, let's see what emotions are associated with greatness and how to cultivate them in real life:

1. Foster Gratitude

You cannot commence your journey towards greatness without being grateful first. That's right, being satisfied with what you already have in life and expressing due gratitude towards it will be your first step towards greatness. Being in a gratified emotional state at most times (if not all) will enhance your mental stability which will consequently help you perceive life in a different—or better point of view. This enhanced perception of life will remove your stresses and allow you to develop beyond the mediocrity of life and towards greatness.

2. Be As Curious As Child

Childhood is the time when a person starts to learn whatever that is around them. A child never stops questioning, a child never runs away from what they have to face. They just deal with things head on. Such kind of eagerness for life is something that most of us lose at the expense of time. As we grow up—as we know more, our interest keeps diminishing. We stop questioning anymore and accept what is. Eventually, we become entrapped into the ordinary. On the contrary, if we greet everything in life with bold eagerness, we expose ourselves to opportunities. And opportunities lead to greatness.

3. Ignite Your Passion

Passion has become a cliché term in any discussion related to achievements and life. Nevertheless, there is no way of denying the role of passion in driving your life force. Your ultimate zeal and fervor towards what you want in life is what distinguishes you to be great. Because admittedly, many people may want the same thing in life but how bad they want it—the intensity of wanting something is what drives people to stand out from the rest and win it over.

4. Become As Persistent As A Mountain

There are two types of great people on earth—1) Those who are born great and 2) Those who persistently work hard to become great. If you're reading this article, you probably belong to the later criteria. Being such, your determination is a key factor towards becoming great. Let nothing obstruct you—remain as firm as a mountain through all thick and thin. That kind of determination is what makes extraordinary out of the ordinary.

5. Develop Adaptability

As I have mentioned earlier, unless you are born great, your journey towards greatness will be an extremely demanding one. You will have to embrace great lengths beyond your comfort. In order to come out successful in such a journey, make sure that you become flexible to unexpected changes in your surroundings. Again, making yourself adaptable first in another journey in itself. You can't make yourself fit in adverse situations immediately. Adaptability or flexibility is cultivated prudently, with time, exposing yourself to adversities, little by little.

6. Confidence Is Key

Road to greatness often means that you have to tread a path that is discouraged by most. It's obvious—by definition, everybody cannot be great. People will most likely advise against you when you aspire something out of the ordinary. Some will even present logical explanations against you;especially your close ones. But nothing should waver your faith. You must remain boldly confident towards what you're pursuing. Only you can bring your greatness. Believe that.

7. Sense of Fulfilment Through Contributions

Honestly, there can be no greater feeling than what you'd feel after your presence has made a real impact on this world. If not, what else do we live for? Having contributed to the world and the people around you; this is the purpose of life. All the big and small contributions you make give meaning to your existence. It connects you to others, man and animal alike. It fulfills your purpose as a human being. We live for this sense of fulfillment and so, become a serial contributor. Create in yourself a greed for this feeling. At the end of the day, those who benefit from your contributions will revere you as great. No amount of success can be compared with this kind of greatness. So, never miss the opportunity of doing a good deed, no matter how minuscule or enormous.

In conclusion, these emotions don't come spontaneously. You have to create these emotions, cultivate them. And to cultivate these emotions, you must first understand yourself and your goals. With your eye on the prize, you have to create these emotions in you which will pave the path to your greatness. Gratitude, curiosity, passion, persistence, adaptability and fulfillment—each has its own weight and with all the emotions at play, nothing can stop you from becoming great in the truest form.